Pride and P
Classroom Questions

A SCENE BY SCENE TEACHING GUIDE

Amy Farrell

SCENE BY SCENE
ENNISKERRY, IRELAND

Scene by Scene
11 Millfield, Enniskerry
Wicklow, Ireland.
www.scenebysceneguides.com

Pride and Prejudice Classroom Questions/Amy Farrell. —1st ed.
ISBN 978-1-910949-22-1

Contents

Chapter One

1. "It is a truth universally acknowledged, that a single man in possession of a good fortune, must be in want of a wife". Comment on the opening line of this novel.

2. What are your first impressions of Mrs. Bennet?

3. What are your first impressions of Mr. Bennet?

Chapter Two

1.   How do the ladies spend their time?

Chapter Three

1.   What kind of man is Mr. Bingley?

2.   What is Mrs. Bennet's primary concern?

3.   What do we learn of Mr. Darcy?

4.   "He was the proudest, most disagreeable man in the world, and every body hoped that he would never come there again."
Why do they feel this way about Mr. Darcy?

5.   "She is tolerable; but not handsome enough to tempt me; and I am in no humour at present to give consequence to young ladies who are slighted by other men."
How would you feel if you were Elizabeth and you overheard this comment?

Chapter Four

1.   How does Jane feel about Mr. Bingley?

2.   What kind of relationship do Jane and Lizzy have?

Chapter Five

1.   What do the women talk about?

Chapter Six

1.   How do the Bennets get on at Netherfield?

2.   Charlotte Lucas tells Lizzy, "In nine cases out of ten, a woman had better shew more affection than she feels. Bingley likes your sister undoubtedly; but he may never do more than like her, if she does not help him on". What do you think of this statement?

3.   Charlotte also tells Lizzy, "Happiness in marriage is entirely a matter of chance....it is better to know as little as possible of the defects of the person with whom you are to pass your life."
Comment on her attitude to marriage.

4.   What do you think of the way characters socialise?

Chapter Seven

1. Why does Mr. Bennet think Catherine and Lydia are "two of the silliest girls in the country."?

2. Why won't Mrs. Bennet let Jane take the carriage to Netherfield?

3. Would you describe Elizabeth and Jane as being close? Explain.

Chapter Eight

1. How do Bingley's sisters view Elizabeth?

2. Mrs. Hurst remarks, "I have an excessive regard for
Jane Bennet, she is really a very sweet girl, and I wish
with all my heart she were well settled. But with such a
father and mother, and such low connections, I am afraid
there is no chance of it."
What do you think of these remarks?

3. Compare Bingley's attitude to the Bennets to that of his
sisters.

4. What does it mean to be an accomplished young lady?

Chapter Nine

1. Why is Mrs. Bennet happy to leave Jane at Netherfield?

2. Darcy remarks, "In a country neighbourhood you move in a very confined and unvarying society". How does he view country society?

3. Why is Elizabeth embarrassed by her mother?

Chapter Ten

1. How does Miss Bingley treat Darcy and why does she treat him like this?

2. How well do Darcy and Lizzy get on, in your opinion?

3. "He really believed, that were it not for the inferiority of her connections, he should be in some danger." Comment on Darcy's thoughts at this point.

Chapter Eleven

1. How are Bingley and Jane getting on?

2. In your opinion, why does Caroline Bingley behave as she does?

3. "My good opinion once lost is lost for ever."
   What kind of man is Darcy, in your opinion?

4. How does Elizabeth view Darcy, in your opinion?

Chapter Twelve

1.   Why is Darcy glad that Jane and Elizabeth are leaving Netherfield?

2.   How do their parents react to their return home?

CLASSROOM QUESTIONS • 13

Chapter Thirteen

1.   Who is this, "gentleman and a stranger," that is visiting
      Longbourn and why is he visiting?

2.   What does the, "entail of the estate," mean for the Bennet
      sisters?

3.   What are your first impressions of Mr. Collins?

Chapter Fourteen

1.   What is Collins' opinion of Lady Catherine de Bourgh?

2.   How does Lydia offend her cousin and how does he react?

Chapter Fifteen

1. "Mr. Collins had only to change from Jane to Elizabeth – and it was soon done – done while Mrs. Bennet was stirring the fire". Explain and comment on this line.

2. "In his library he had always been sure of leisure and tranquillity". What kind of man is Mr. Bennet, in your opinion?

3. Describe Mr. Wickham.

4. How do Mr. Darcy and Mr. Wickham react when they see one another?

Chapter Sixteen

1. How well do Elizabeth and Mr. Wickham get on?

2. What is Wickham's view of Mr. Darcy?

3. What information does Mr. Wickham provide Elizabeth with about Darcy?

4. What is Wickham's view of Miss Darcy?

5. What information does Wickham have about Miss de Bourgh?

Chapter Seventeen

1.   How does Jane react to Elizabeth's tale of Darcy and
        Wickham?

2.   What various reasons do the Bennets have for looking
        forward to Mr. Bingley's ball?

3.   Why is Mr. Collins so friendly to Elizabeth, in her opinion?

Chapter Eighteen

1.   "She was resolved against any sort of conversation with him, and turned away with a degree of ill humour". Why does Elizabeth treat Darcy this way?

2.   Why were Elizabeth's first two dances, "dances of mortification"?

3.   How well do Elizabeth and Mr. Darcy get on, in your opinion?

4.   How does Mr. Darcy react to the mention of Mr. Wickham?

5.   Why does Mr. Collins want to meet Mr. Darcy?

6.   Why was Elizabeth "vexed" at dinner?

7.   Describe Mrs. Bennet.

8.   What kind of evening did Elizabeth have?

Chapter Nineteen

1. What does Mr. Collins do?

2. What are his reasons for marrying?

3. How does Elizabeth react to his proposal?

4. Why does Mr. Collins intend to propose again?

5. How would you react if you were Elizabeth?

Chapter Twenty

1.   How does Mrs. Bennet react to Lizzy's decision?

2.   How does Mr. Bennet react to the news of Collins' proposal?

Chapter Twenty One

1. What reason does Mr. Wickham give for missing the ball at Netherfield?

2. What news does Caroline Bingley's letter contain?

3. "Indeed, Jane, you ought to believe me. No one who has ever seen you together, can doubt his affection."
    What does Elizabeth think Caroline Bingley is up to?

Chapter Twenty Two

1.   Why are Charlotte Lucas' parents agreeable when Mr.
      Collins proposes?

2.   How does Charlotte view her future marriage to
      Mr. Collins?

3.   How does Elizabeth react to Charlotte's news?

4.   "But when you have had time to think it all over, I hope
      you will be satisfied with what I have done."
      How does Charlotte explain accepting Mr. Collins'
      proposal to Elizabeth?

Chapter Twenty Three

1. How does Mrs. Bennet react to news of the engagement?

2. "The sight of Miss Lucas was odious to her."
   What is Mrs. Bennet's main problem with Charlotte?

Chapter Twenty Four

1. What different views do Jane and Elizabeth have of Charlotte's marriage?

2. Why does Jane think she was mistaken in thinking Mr. Bingley was interested in her?

Chapter Twenty Five

1.   Why does Elizabeth feel Jane will not bump into Mr. Bingley in London?

2.   How do Elizabeth and Mrs. Gardiner refer to Mr. Darcy in this chapter?

Chapter Twenty Six

1. Why aren't Elizabeth and Charlotte as close as they once were?

2. How does Caroline Bingley treat Jane in this chapter?

3. "His apparent partiality had subsided." Why is Wickham now giving so much attention to someone else?

4. Is Elizabeth upset by Wickham's disinterest? Why?

Chapter Twenty Seven

1.   What view does Mrs. Gardiner have of Mr. Wickham?

2.   What invitation do the Gardiners make to Lizzy?

Chapter Twenty Eight

1.   Do you think Charlotte and Mr. Collins' marriage is a
      successful one?

2.   Describe Miss De Bourgh.

Chapter Twenty Nine

1.   What comment does Mr. Collins make about Elizabeth's clothes?

2.   How do the visitors react to meeting Lady Catherine?

3.   What is Lady Catherine like?

4.   What activities does Lady Catherine think young ladies should participate in?

Chapter Thirty

1.   Why doesn't Charlotte use the dining parlour for common use?

2.   What is Charlotte's life like at the Parsonage?

3.   What reason does Charlotte think up for Darcy visiting?

Chapter Thirty One

1.   How does Lady Catherine de Bourgh react to Elizabeth
     and Colonel Fitzwilliam's conversation?

2.   What excuses does Darcy give Colonel Fitzwilliam for
     dancing only four dances when Elizabeth first met him?

3.   Does Elizabeth think Darcy is interested in Miss de Bourgh?

Chapter Thirty Two

1.   What information does Mr. Darcy give Elizabeth about Mr. Bingley's intentions to return to Netherfield?

2.   What reason does Charlotte interpret for Darcy's visit to the Parsonage?

Chapter Thirty Three

1. Does Elizabeth enjoy unexpectedly meeting Mr. Darcy when she's out walking?

2. Colonel Fitzwilliam tells Elizabeth that Darcy, "congratulated himself on having lately saved a friend from the inconveniences of a most imprudent marriage." How does Elizabeth react to this?

Chapter Thirty Four

1. "Colonel Fitzwilliam had made it clear that he had no intentions at all". What does this line mean?

2. "You must allow me to tell you how ardently I admire and love you". How does Elizabeth react to Darcy's profession of love?

3. Does Darcy make this statement in a romantic fashion, in your opinion?

4. What reasons does Elizabeth give for rejecting him?

5. "Could you expect me to rejoice in the inferiority of your connections?" How would you react to this comment if you were Elizabeth?

Chapter Thirty Five

1.   Why was Darcy walking in the grove that morning?
      What do you think of this?

2.   What does Darcy have to say about the situation with
      Jane and Mr. Bingley?

3.   What does Darcy say about Mr. Wickham in his letter?

4.   How would you feel after reading this letter if you were
      Elizabeth?

Chapter Thirty Six

1.   What does Elizabeth begin to realise about Wickham?

2.   How does Elizabeth feel as the chapter ends?

Chapter Thirty Seven

1.   What does Lady Catherine want Elizabeth to do?

2.   What does the reference to servants tell you?

3.   What view does Elizabeth have of her own family?

Chapter Thirty Eight

1.   How does Mr. Collins view his marriage to Charlotte?

2.   Did Maria enjoy the trip?

3.   Why is Elizabeth unsure about what she should reveal to Jane as the chapter ends?

Chapter Thirty Nine

1.   What news does Lydia have about Mr. Wickham?

2.   "Have you seen any pleasant men? Have you had any
     flirting? I was in great hopes that one of you would have
     got a husband before you came back. Jane will be quite an
     old maid soon, I declare." Describe Lydia's character.

3.   What is the "Brighton scheme" that Elizabeth's parents are
     discussing and what does it tell you about them?

Chapter Forty

1. How does Jane respond to Elizabeth's news of Darcy's proposal and the newfound information concerning Wickham?

2. "At present I will say nothing about it."
   Why does Elizabeth decide against revealing the truth about Wickham?
   What would you do in her situation?

3. What does Elizabeth keep from Jane?
   Do you understand why she does this?

4. What does Mrs. Bennet accuse the Collinses of talking about constantly?

Chapter Forty One

1. Why are Kitty and Lydia miserable?

2. What good news does Lydia receive?

3. What problem does Elizabeth have with Lydia?

4. Why is Mr. Bennet unconcerned about Lydia?

5. How does Elizabeth treat Wickham when she sees him at dinner and why does she mention Colonel Forster and Mr. Darcy?

Chapter Forty Two

1. What does the narrator reveal to us about the Bennets' marriage?

2. What does Elizabeth look forward to?

3. How do the plans change?

4. Why does Elizabeth want to avoid going to Pemberley?

Chapter Forty Three

1. "At that moment she felt, that to be mistress of Pemberley might be something!" Comment on this line.

2. Why is Elizabeth surprised by the housekeeper's opinion of Darcy?

3. What effect do the housekeeper's words have on Elizabeth?

4. "She was over-powered by shame and vexation." Why does Elizabeth feel this way?

5. What surprises Elizabeth about Darcy's behaviour?

6. "She was flattered and pleased." What does Darcy ask Elizabeth that makes her feel this way?

7. What do Elizabeth's aunt and uncle think of Mr. Darcy?

Chapter Forty Four

1.   What do Elizabeth's aunt and uncle make of Darcy and his sister visiting them so soon?

2.   What does Elizabeth find encouraging about Bingley's behaviour?

3.   "She lay awake two whole hours." Why can't Elizabeth sleep?

Chapter Forty Five

1.   How does Miss Bingley treat Elizabeth when they meet in Pemberley?

2.   "But Georgiana would not join her." Why doesn't Georgiana join in when Miss Bingley criticises Elizabeth?

3.   When provoked, what does Darcy reveal to Miss Bingley about his thoughts on Elizabeth?
      What do you think about this?

4.   "They talked of his sister, his friends, his house, his fruit, of every thing but himself; yet Elizabeth was longing to know what Mrs. Gardiner thought of him, and Mrs. Gardiner would have been highly gratified by her niece's beginning the subject."
      How must Elizabeth be feeling at this stage?

5.   Could you cope with keeping everything to yourself in a situation like this?

Chapter Forty Six

1.   What news does Jane's letter reveal about Lydia?

2.   "Imprudent as a marriage between Mr. Wickham and our
     poor Lydia would be, we are now anxious to be assured
     it has taken place…" Why are the family concerned that
     Lydia has *not* married Wickham?

3.   What is your opinion of Mr. Wickham at this stage?

4.   "Never had she so honestly felt that she could have loved
     him, as now, when all love must be vain."
     What makes Elizabeth think that Mr. Darcy is beyond
     her reach?

5.   "Sometimes one officer, sometimes another had been
     her favourite." What do you think of Lydia's behaviour in
     this elopement?

Chapter Forty Seven

1.   Why does Mr. Gardiner believe he is right to "hope the best" about Lydia?

2.   "Wickham will never marry a woman without some money. He cannot afford it."
        Comment on this line and what image it creates of marriage in the novel.

3.   What do you think of the idea that Lydia running away with Wickham is a scandalous disgrace?
        Would people react the same way now?

4.   Who does Mrs. Bennet blame for Lydia's elopement?

5.   "If they are not married already, make them marry."
        Comment on the thinking behind this, considering the unsuitability of the match.

6.   Comment on the tone of Lydia's note.

7.   "Under such a misfortune as this, one cannot see too little of one's neighbours." Comment on this line.

Chapter Forty Eight

1. "All Meryton seemed striving to blacken the man, who, but three months before, had been almost an angel of light. He was declared to be in debt to every tradesman in the place...he was the wickedest young man in the world..."
   How has your opinion of Wickham been changed?

2. "The death of your daughter would have been a blessing in comparison of this."
   Comment on this line in Mr. Collins' letter.

Chapter Forty Nine

1. In Mr. Gardiner's letter he outlines conditions that must be met before Wickham and Lydia marry. What are these conditions?

2. Why does Mr. Bennet think Mr. Gardiner has already paid off Wickham?

3. "In a short time, I shall have a daughter married. Mrs. Wickham! How well it sounds."
   Do you think Mrs. Bennet is too quick to decide this is good news?

Chapter Fifty

1. According to Mr. Bennet, why didn't he set money aside for, "the better provision of his children, and of his wife, if she survived him"?

2. "With such an husband, her misery was considered certain." Do you feel sorry for Lydia because of the way people view her marriage?

3. "Into one house in this neighbourhood, they shall never have admittance." Do you think Mr. Bennet is judging Lydia and Wickham too harshly?

4. "What a triumph for him, as she often thought, could he know that the proposals which she had proudly spurned only four months ago, would now have been gladly and gratefully received!" Explain Elizabeth's change of heart.

5. "She began now to comprehend that he was exactly the man, who, in disposition and talents, would most suit her." How must Elizabeth be feeling at this stage?

6. Are you surprised that Mr. Bennet consents to having Lydia and Wickham visit Longbourn?

Chapter Fifty One

1. How do Lydia and Wickham behave when they arrive at Longbourn?

2. "Wickham's affection for Lydia, was what Elizabeth had expected to find it; not equal to Lydia's for him."
    Do you feel sorry for Lydia?
    What "secret" does Lydia let slip to Elizabeth?

3. "Jane's delicate sense of honour would not allow her to speak to Elizabeth privately of what Lydia had let fall." Comment on this lack of open discussion.

Chapter Fifty Two

1.   Why did Mr. Darcy help to find Mr. Wickham?

2.   "Wickham of course wanted more than he could get; but at length was reduced to be reasonable". What do you think of Wickham negotiating a marriage deal?

3.   What reason does Mrs. Gardiner hint at for Darcy being so helpful in this situation?

4.   How does Elizabeth react to this letter?

5.   "Come, Mr. Wickham, we are brother and sister, you know. Do not let us quarrel about the past."
      Do you think Elizabeth really means this? Explain.

Chapter Fifty Three

1. "But you know married women have never much time for writing. My sisters may write to me. They will have nothing else to do." Comment on Lydia's statement.

2. What news arrives concerning Netherfield?

3. How does Jane feel about this news?

4. How do Jane and Elizabeth act when the men arrive?

5. How do the men behave?

6. "She was in no humour for conversation with any one but himself; and to him she had hardly courage to speak." Do you understand how Elizabeth feels?

7. Why is Elizabeth embarrassed by her mother in this chapter?

Chapter Fifty Four

1.   Do you believe Jane when she says, "You must not suspect me", regarding Bingley?

Chapter Fifty Five

1. Why does Mrs. Bennet want Jane left on her own with Mr. Bingley?

2. Does Mr. Bingley get on well with Mrs. Bennet?

3. Why is Jane, "the happiest creature in the world"?

4. Why has Mr. Bingley gone to see Mr. Bennet immediately?

5. "The Bennets were speedily pronounced to be the luckiest family in the world." Do you think the business with Lydia and Wickham has been forgotten rather quickly?

Chapter Fifty Six

1. What "scandalous falsehood" does Lady Catherine want to discuss with Elizabeth?

2. "You may have drawn him in."
   What is your opinion of Lady Catherine's behaviour?

3. Do you think Elizabeth handles the situation well?

4. "If you were sensible of your own good, you would not wish to quit the sphere, in which you have been brought up." What is Lady Catherine saying here?

Chapter Fifty Seven

1. "With his notions of dignity, he would probably feel that
    the arguments, which to Elizabeth had appeared weak and
    ridiculous, contained much good sense and solid
    reasoning." What is Elizabeth afraid of?

2. How does Mr. Bennet react to Mr. Collins' hint that
    Darcy is interested in Elizabeth?

3. "So delightfully absurd!" How does Elizabeth feel because
    of her father's reaction?

Chapter Fifty Eight

1. What reason does Darcy give for helping Lydia?

2. What is your opinion of Darcy at this stage?

3. What was the effect of Lady Catherine's attempt to block the match?

4. "What do I not owe you!"
   What does Darcy feel he owes Elizabeth?

Chapter Fifty Nine

1.   How does Jane react to Elizabeth's news?

2.   "Oh Lizzy! do any thing rather than marry without affection." Comment on this advice.

3.   "It has been coming on so gradually, that I hardly know when it began. But I believe I must date it from my first seeing his beautiful grounds at Pemberley."
   How do you interpret this line?

4.   What makes Mrs. Bennet seem stupid in this chapter?

5.   "We all know him to be a proud, unpleasant sort of man; but this would be nothing if you really liked him."
   Comment on Mr. Bennet's statement.

6.   When Mrs. Bennet hears Lizzy's news, what does she immediately think of?

Chapter Sixty

1.   What is the tone in this chapter?

Chapter Sixty One

1.   What do you think of Lydia's letter to Lizzy?

2.   "His affection for her soon sunk into indifference."
Are you surprised that Lydia and Wickham's marriage is problematic?

3.   Do you like the ending? Explain.

Visit www.scenebysceneguides.com to see our full catalogue of
Classroom Questions and Workbooks.

Hamlet Scene by Scene Classroom Questions

Romeo and Juliet Scene by Scene Classroom Questions

King Lear Scene by Scene Classroom Questions

Macbeth Scene by Scene Classroom Questions

A Doll's House Classroom Questions

Animal Farm Classroom Questions

Foster Classroom Questions

Good Night, Mr. Tom Classroom Questions

Subscribe to our newsletter to keep up to date with all the latest title releases at www.scenebysceneguides.com/newsletter

Martyn Pig Classroom Questions

Of Mice and Men Classroom Questions

Pride and Prejudice Classroom Questions

Private Peaceful Classroom Questions

The Fault in Our Stars Classroom Questions

The Old Man and the Sea Classroom Questions

The Outsiders Classroom Questions

To Kill a Mockingbird Classroom Questions

The Spinning Heart Classroom Questions

Lightning Source UK Ltd.
Milton Keynes UK
UKOW06f0127131015

260413UK00008B/142/P